GOOD DRINKS
DRINKS
for
BAD
DAYS

Kerry Colburn

SASQUATCH
BOOKS

For Rob, who always knows exactly how
to fix a bad day (and a perfect Manhattan).

Printed in Canada
Published by Sasquatch Books
Distributed by PGW/Perseus
15 14 13 12 11 10 09 08   10 9 8 7 6 5 4 3 2 1

Cover illustration: Kate Quinby
Cover design: Henry Quiroga
Interior design: Henry Quiroga
Interior illustrations: Kate Quinby

Library of Congress Cataloging-in-Publication Data

Colburn, Kerry.
  Good drinks for bad days / Kerry Colburn. -- 1st ed.
     p. cm.
ISBN-13: 978-1-57061-555-9
ISBN-10: 1-57061-555-1
1. Cocktails. 2. Cocktails--Humor. 3. Fortune--Humor. I. Title.
TX951.C7225 2008
641.8'74--dc22

                          2008022779

Sasquatch Books
119 South Main Street, Suite 400
Seattle, WA 98104
(206) 467-4300

www.sasquatchbooks.com
custserv@sasquatchbooks.com

TABLE *of* CONTENTS

Introduction . . . vii

Glassware & Garnishes . . . viii

Bad Days: Work . . . 1

Nightmare commute • *Irish Coffee*
Bombed interview • *B-52*
Heinous meeting • *Death in the Afternoon*
Humiliated self at office party • *Mind Eraser*
Got fired • *Flaming Diablo*
Annoying coworker got the promotion • *Stinger*
New job blues • *Blue Hawaiian*
Assistant quit • *Mudslide*
No raise • *Greenback*
Computer virus • *Hot Toddy*
Presentation from hell • *Kamikaze*
Monday • *Bellini*

Bad Days: Love . . . 27

Ran into evil ex • *French 75*
Hooked up with totally wrong person • *Tequila Sunrise*
Bumped into crush while looking awful • *Beautiful*
Stood up • *Whiskey Sour*
Awful blind date • *Love Potion*
Wedding invitation from former flame • *Champagne Cocktail*
Bad sex • *Between the Sheets*
Big fight with main squeeze • *Short Fuse*
Worst kiss ever • *French Kiss*
Stolen date • *Barracuda*
Struck out • *South of the Border*
Best friend is in love • *Honeymoon*
Ugly breakup • *Death by Chocolate*

Bad Days: Home ... 55

Noisy neighbors kept you up all night • *Harvey Wallbanger*
Rent hike • *Manhattan*
Household disaster • *Rusty Nail*
Cable on the fritz • *Zombie*
Cleaning day • *Dirty Martini*
Cranky relatives staying with you • *Quaalude*
Moving day • *Black Magic*
Screwed over by roommate • *Screwdriver*
Actually home sick on sick day • *Blueberry Tea*
Party aftermath • *Sea Breeze*

Bad Days: Life in General ... 77

Car broke down • *Greyhound*
Flight cancelled • *Hurricane*
Fashion faux pas • *Black and Tan*
Got arrested • *Alabama Slammer*
Called "sir" or "ma'am" by teenage salesclerk • *Vodka Red Bull*
Totally unfair speeding ticket • *Sloe Gin Fizz*
Hangover • *Red Eye*
Buyer's remorse • *Mimosa*
Tax day • *Cuba Libre*
Gained weight • *Butterball*
Sold out by friend • *Bloody Caesar*
Got into a fight • *Planter's Punch*
Crummy birthday • *Irish Cream Milkshake*
Painful grooming treatment • *Fuzzy Navel*
Sports team got crushed • *Salty Dog*
Miserable weather • *Dark and Stormy*
Last-minute holiday shopping • *Hot Buttered Rum*
Fender bender • *Sidecar*

Index ... 115

Introduction

No matter how you slice it, some days are just losers. You can put forth your best effort, try to keep your chin up, channel inner peace, and still—wham! Life comes up and smacks you upside the head. Others might give you all sorts of advice for how to deal with the ugly and unfair mishaps that befall you: meditation, jogging, being "zen" about it. They might offer you nuggets of wisdom like "tomorrow's another day" or "better luck next time" or "got to take the bad with the good." Yeah, right! The reality is, when the day really sucks, forget about all the ways you might rise above it—you have the right to wallow in it.

In this book you'll find more than 50 delicious antidotes for myriad miserable circumstances. If your boss has screwed you over, your date is a disaster, your rent's gone up again, or your car broke down on the freeway, make the most of it—make a drink out of it! Look up your bad day in this book—handily organized by Work, Love, Home, and Life in General—and find the magic recipe to make it all better. You can rest assured that drowning your sorrows in a potent and perfectly paired cocktail will counteract any everyday disaster better and faster than yoga, therapy, or the power of positive thinking. You may have had a bad day, but here's to a much better night.

So open the liquor cabinet, get out the good glasses, and mix away. Tell yourself your problems and give yourself some much-deserved sympathy. Make yourself another round on the house. You deserve it! Soon you'll be your own best bartender, the one who can really cure whatever ails you. And that's a very good skill to have on any very bad day.

Bottoms up!

Glassware & Garnishes

Let's get one thing straight: there are days so heinous that what you drink (and how quickly you can fix it) is infinitely more important than what you drink it out of. On those occasions, a strong martini with no olives in a marginally clean plastic cup might be just fine. But, when possible, the proper glass and garnish can elevate your cocktail—and your mood. So, if you've got access to the proper tools in your house, treat yourself to a nicely executed beverage now and then—God knows you deserve it. Here are some bar basics to help you along:

Glassware

Champagne flute [🍸]: Designed with a tall, narrow opening to retain effervescence, this is the glass of choice for any bubbly cocktail.

Cocktail glass [🍸]: Also called a martini glass, this sophisticated stemmed glass is the one to use for shaken or stirred cocktails.

Highball glass [🥛]: Also called a Collins glass, this tall, straight-sided glass is the most versatile for your bar, perfect for any long drink (and for making short drinks into long drinks).

Old-fashioned glass [🥃]: Another handy glass to have on hand, this one is short and stout with a heavy bottom, ideal for any drink on the rocks. (Also called a rocks glass, tumbler, or whiskey glass; the larger version is a double old-fashioned.)

Shot glass [🥃]: For cutting to the chase, there's no substitute for a shot, no chaser. This two-ounce bad boy is your go-to glass when even ice seems extraneous.

Wine glass [🍷]: Any wine glass, especially a larger goblet-style one, is a nice choice for punch or any tropical or frozen drink. It can also be used as a change of scene for a highball.

Beer mug [🍺]: 'Nuff said. (To take it up a notch, put it in the freezer before using.)

Pint glass [🍺]: This tapered, pint-size glass with no handle is usually reserved for beer or hard cider (it's best not to use a pint glass for a mixed drink unless you really mean business).

Brandy snifter [🥃]: This short-stemmed glass with its very round bowl is ideal for swirling and sniffing the good stuff—brandy, liqueurs, and Cognacs—and for feeling superior.

Garnishes

Most garnishes are straightforward: just slice a wedge of lime or grab a few raspberries and toss them in your drink. But here's a quick primer for when you're going a bit more highbrow.

Twist: If a drink calls for a twist, use a paring knife to cut an approximately 2-inch strip of peel from a washed piece of citrus, avoiding as much of the pith as possible. Twist the peel just above the drink, then run it around the rim (if desired) and drop it in.

Spiral: A longer version of the twist, this streamer-like curlicue adds festive panache to a cocktail. Use a vegetable peeler or paring knife to remove a thin, continuous peel from one end of the fruit to the other, then twist it around your finger and drop it in the drink.

Slices and wheels: When a drink calls for a fruit slice or wheel, use a sharp paring knife to cut off the end of the fruit and then cut a crosswise segment about ¼ inch wide. To use as a garnish, cut a slice in the wheel and balance on the side of the glass.

Salted or sugared rims: To salt or sugar a rim, coat the rim of the glass with a citrus wedge and then dunk it onto a small plate or bowl of salt or superfine sugar. Turn gently to distribute, shake off any excess, and then carefully pour in your cocktail.

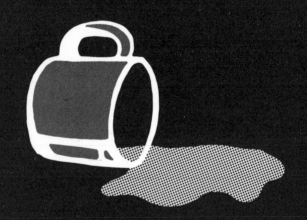

BAD DAYS: WORK

Bad Day: *Nightmare commute*

What better use for your commuter mug than to hold a delightful traffic-angst antidote? (We're talking once you're safely home, of course.) If you dealt with traffic today that made you bang the steering wheel, make obscene gestures, or contemplate moving to rural Iowa, you deserve more in your mug than humdrum French Roast. Make it all better with a cup of Joe like only the Irish can make!

Good Drink: *Irish Coffee*

1½ ounces Irish whiskey
1 teaspoon brown sugar
6 ounces strong hot coffee
Heavy cream or whipped cream

Pour the whiskey into your warmed commuter mug, add the brown sugar, and stir until dissolved. Pour in the hot coffee. Slowly add the cream to float on top, or top with whipped cream (or both).

From Bad to Worse: **Had to endure that commute while carpooling with an annoying coworker? Double the whiskey and use half the coffee.**

Bad Day: *Bombed interview*

Did you stutter? Forget where you went to college? Arrive late? Burp? Say something really, really dumb? Accidentally insult the interviewer? No matter. A cocktail named for an even more infamous bomber will make you start to believe that it wasn't the job for you anyway. Here's to bigger, better opportunities ahead—bombs away!

Good Drink: *B-52*

   ½ ounce Kahlúa
   ½ ounce Baileys or other Irish cream liqueur
   ½ ounce Grand Marnier

Slowly pour the Kahlúa, Baileys, and Grand Marnier, in that order, into a chilled glass. Sip while creatively embellishing your resumé.

Bad Day: *Heinous meeting*

When it's 3 p.m., your blood sugar is dangerously low, and quitting time seems oh-so-far away, there's nothing worse than a truly excruciating meeting. Whether it's a painful Power-Point presentation, a bunch of senseless squabbling, or just an unbelievably boring agenda, you can doodle, zone out, and envision the perfect cocktail that will be yours as soon as this nightmare ends. (By the way, this drink is also known as the Hemingway . . . do you think that guy *ever* had to sit for two hours in a stuffy conference room?)

Good Drink: *Death in the Afternoon*

½ ounce Pernod
5 ounces chilled champagne

Pour the Pernod into a chilled champagne flute. Swirl it to coat the inside of the glass, and slowly top with champagne.

From Bad to Worse: **Meeting goes into overtime and the boss calls for an adjournment until *Saturday*? Go big and use absinthe in place of Pernod—you won't even know you were there.**

Bad Day: *Humiliated self at office party*

There's something about office parties that makes people go a little crazy. Perhaps you drank a *wee* bit too much, told your boss how you really feel about a new policy, or found yourself in a compromising position in the supply closet. Maybe you showed off some dance moves and karaoke stylings that really should have been left in the privacy of your own bedroom. Regardless, people are probably talking. Call in sick today and ease your pain with a drink that will help you forget it ever happened . . . in a couple of days, they will too.

Good Drink: *Mind Eraser*

½ ounce Kahlúa
1½ ounces vodka
3 ounces club soda

Pour the Kahlúa into an ice-filled glass. Gently float the vodka
on top, then slowly top with club soda. Don't stir. Think happy
thoughts and practice saying, "Party? What party?"

From Bad to Worse: **Leave incriminating evidence in the copy machine? Add a shot
of Grand Marnier.**

Bad Day: *Got fired*

When you get fired, you've just gotta light something on fire. And while you might be tempted to torch your desk, your files, your boss's car, or your business suit, it's much more therapeutic—and enjoyable, not to mention legal—to set a drink on fire. Burn, baby, burn!

Good Drink: *Flaming Diablo*

1 ounce Cognac
½ ounce Cointreau
2 whole cloves
1 long strip of lemon peel
1 long strip of orange peel
6 ounces hot coffee

In a saucepan over medium heat, combine the Cognac, Cointreau, cloves, lemon peel, and orange peel. Pour the coffee into a heat-resistant mug and set aside. As bubbles form along the edge of the pan, stand back and use a long-handled match to ignite the booze, using extreme caution (never add more alcohol once the concoction is aflame). Pour the flaming mixture into the coffee mug while saying a curse on those bastards who wronged you.

Bad Day: *Annoying coworker got the promotion*

So much for "may the better man win." The truth is, sometimes the most irritating, idea-stealing, brown-nosing, long-lunch-taking man or woman wins—and it's painful to watch. If it's a promotion that really should've gone to you, that *really* stings. Ouch!

Good Drink: *Stinger*

> *1½ ounces brandy*
> *1½ ounces white crème de menthe*

Stir the brandy and crème de menthe with ice and strain into a chilled cocktail glass, or shake and pour into an ice-filled old-fashioned glass.

From Bad to Worse: Now you have to report to this moron? Make it a White Spider Stinger: a hearty 2 ounces of vodka plus ¾ ounce of either white crème de menthe or peppermint schnapps, prepped the same way.

Bad Day: *New job blues*

It's never quite what they promise you, is it? Sometimes what seems to be a fab new job on paper leaves a little to be desired—especially during those first few days. Your phone isn't hooked up, your desk is filthy, and no one is around to show you where anything is. And besides all that, a pile of overdue work has been left behind by your clearly incompetent predecessor. If your first day on the job feels like the first day of school times ten, it's time to escape with a decadent drink that will make you feel the opposite of blue.

Good Drink: *Blue Hawaiian*

1 ounce light rum
1 ounce blue curaçao
1 ounce cream of coconut
2 ounces pineapple juice
Pineapple wedge and maraschino cherry for garnish

Shake the rum, curaçao, cream of coconut, and pineapple juice with ice and strain into an ice-filled highball glass (or combine with ½ cup ice in blender and blend until smooth for a frozen version). Garnish with the pineapple and cherry.

Bad Day: *Assistant quit*

If you're lucky enough to have an assistant, not to mention a hard-working one, it's a disastrous day indeed when he or she leaves you. Suddenly, you have a mountain of mail, a wall of mysterious-looking files, and a towering stack of unread reports all caving in on you. It looks like a big, messy heap of trouble is barreling straight toward your office. Run for your life—before you get buried!

Good Drink: *Mudslide*

1 ounce vodka
1 ounce Kahlúa
1 ounce Baileys or other Irish cream liqueur
1 ounce heavy cream
Unsweetened cocoa powder or chocolate shavings for garnish

Shake the vodka, Kahlúa, Baileys, and heavy cream with ice and strain into a chilled cocktail glass (or combine ingredients in blender with ½ cup ice for a frozen version). Sprinkle with cocoa powder. Drink with a pile of resumés on the side.

Bad Day: *No raise*

You've finally made it through another year at your job, and the only thing you're looking forward to is a few extra bucks to make it all worthwhile. But during your review you start hearing terms like "cost-cutting measures" and "wage freeze," and you start kissing that extra dough goodbye. When you realize that your paltry "cost of living increase" will barely cover the cost of a decent lunch, you need to score some greenbacks—and fast.

Good Drink: *Greenback*

1½ ounces gin
¼ ounce crème de menthe
½ ounce fresh lime juice
2 to 3 ounces chilled club soda

Shake the gin, crème de menthe, and lime juice with ice and strain into an ice-filled glass. Top with club soda.

From Bad to Worse: **Didn't even get the cost of living bump? Skip the club soda, and make it a double.**

Bad Day: *Computer virus*

Are you kidding me? You open one innocent-looking e-mail attachment and suddenly, your archives are corrupted, two weeks' worth of spreadsheets have gone missing, and everyone in your address book has received a potentially lethal e-mail from you. Augh! Will your trusted computer ever be the same? The only way to nurse it (and yourself) back to health is with a soothing (and stiff) drink that's been working wonders since long before NyQuil. Get well soon!

Good Drink: *Hot Toddy*

3 whole cloves
Lemon slice
1 teaspoon brown sugar
Pinch of nutmeg
1½ ounces bourbon
6 ounces boiling water
1 cinnamon stick

Push the cloves into the lemon slice and drop into a warmed mug. Add the sugar, nutmeg, and bourbon. Pour in the boiling water, and stir with the cinnamon stick. Put on your most comfy pj's, place an ice pack on your head, and enjoy.

Bad Day: *Presentation from hell*

It's happened to the best of us, and this time it's your turn: you went down in flames in front of all your coworkers. Sure, maybe you could've prepped a bit better. Or maybe it's entirely the fault of your evil assistant, the idiot at Kinko's, or the diabolical PowerPoint software. Whatever the cause, it was not your finest hour. Block out the pain of being shot down in the conference room with this high-octane drink.

Good Drink: *Kamikaze*

2 ounces vodka
½ ounce Cointreau or triple sec
¼ ounce fresh lime juice

Shake the vodka, Cointreau, and lime juice with ice, and strain into a chilled cocktail glass.

From Bad to Worse: Did you actually get heckled? Make it a shooter: change all the measurements above to ³/₄ ounce, dump into a shot glass, and knock it back. Repeat.

Bad Day: *Monday*

Sometimes, nothing in particular happens to make it an especially bad day. The alarm goes off and you're instantly depressed. People annoy you. Nothing seems interesting. Your outlook is bleak and your mood grim. It's just a Monday— another Monday in a long line of Mondays. What can possibly break the spell? Well, bubbly, of course! And ask any Italian: there's nothing like a Bellini to make you feel swell in a hurry. Cheers to Tuesday!

Good Drink: *Bellini*

3 ounces peach purée or peach nectar
4 to 6 ounces chilled Prosecco or any other dry sparkling
* wine or champagne*
Peach slice for garnish

Pour the peach purée into a chilled champagne flute. Slowly add the Prosecco, stirring gently. Garnish with the peach slice.

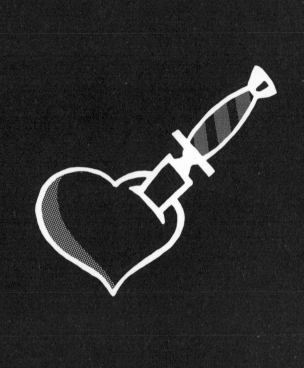

BAD DAYS:
LOVE

Bad Day: *Ran into evil ex*

Oh, what the French know about love and revenge. Named for a French gun used in World War I, this cocktail has vicious roots—making it ideal for combating baddies. Throw some darts at your ex's picture while drinking this decadent drink, and then remember what they say about living well. *C'est vrai!*

Good Drink: *French 75*

1 ounce gin
½ ounce fresh lemon juice
1 teaspoon sugar
5 ounces chilled champagne
Orange peel spiral for garnish

Shake the gin, lemon juice, and sugar with ice, and strain into a highball glass or champagne flute. Slowly top with champagne. Garnish with the orange peel spiral. *Voilà!*

Bad Day: *Hooked up with totally wrong person*

It was an innocent mistake, surely. But somehow, last night you accidentally made out with a coworker, boss, ex, friend's love interest, or just someone you're not interested in seeing again—*ever*. Erase the painful images of an inappropriate evening with a tried-and-true dose of sunshine, and you'll be ready to face the day.

Good Drink: *Tequila Sunrise*

1½ ounces tequila
6 ounces orange juice
½ ounce grenadine or Chambord
2 ounces club soda (optional)

Stir the tequila and orange juice in an ice-filled highball glass. Float the grenadine on top and let it slowly flow through the drink. Top with club soda, if desired.

From Bad to Worse: Still there in the morning? Couldn't find your car keys? Missing an article of clothing? Oh, my. Cut the extraneous ingredients; you'll need straight tequila for the walk of shame.

Bad Day: *Bumped into crush while looking awful*

You've been waiting for weeks to run into that hottie from your building, bus, or neighborhood. Of course, it happens today, when you're fighting a nasty cold, wearing your worst sweats, and haven't showered in three days. Time to wallow with a drink that will make you feel elevated to a better, more attractive place. And hey, look on the bright side—maybe next time you won't even be recognized as the troll who said "hi" today!

Good Drink: *Beautiful*

1 ounce Cognac
1 ounce Grand Marnier

Pour the Cognac and Grand Marnier into a brandy snifter.
Don't stir. Just drink.

From Bad to Worse: Realized you still have zit cream on your face? Add a shot of amaretto to the mix.

Bad Day: *Stood up*

You got cleaned up. You were on time. You stood at the bar for an hour. But no sign of your supposed date. What kind of a person does that? No one you want to spend time with, surely. Get rid of that bitter taste with something strong and sour—and unlike your missing date, something worthy of your own sweet mouth.

Good Drink: *Whiskey Sour*

2 ounces whiskey
¾ ounce fresh lemon juice
½ ounce simple syrup*
Lemon or orange wheel for garnish
Maraschino cherry for garnish

Shake the whiskey, lemon juice, and simple syrup with ice.
Either strain into a chilled glass or serve over ice. Garnish
with the lemon wheel and cherry, and let yourself be a sour-
puss for the rest of the evening.

*Make the simple syrup by stirring 2 parts granulated sugar into 1 part
hot water and letting the sugar dissolve completely. Cool before using.

Bad Day: *Awful blind date*

You finally, *finally* got talked into a fix-up—by your friend, your mother, or an Internet site. Bad idea! Instead of the fantastic, fascinating eligible that was described to you, you spent three painful hours with a total bore—*and* you got stuck with the bill. The only remedy now is a comfy couch, some bad TV, and a drink that promises much better dates to come.

Good Drink: *Love Potion*

1½ ounces lemon-flavored vodka
¾ ounce Chambord
¾ ounce cranberry juice

Shake the vodka, Chambord, and cranberry juice vigorously
with ice and strain into a chilled cocktail glass. Drink while
watching reruns of *Blind Date* on cable.

Bad Day: *Wedding invitation from former flame*

Somehow, a former big love of your life has found The One—and, unbelievably, it isn't you. Worse, it's some loser you don't even like. When you get an invitation like this in the mail, it's best to raise a glass to yourself, giving a wedding-worthy toast that covers all your best qualities. Then start working on securing the hottest possible date for the occasion. Cheers to the single life!

Good Drink: *Champagne Cocktail*

1 sugar cube
2 to 3 dashes Angostura bitters
4 ounces chilled dry champagne
Lemon twist for garnish

Soak the sugar cube in the bitters at the bottom of a chilled champagne flute. Slowly top with champagne. Run the lemon peel around the rim, twist, and drop it in.

From Bad to Worse: Not even allowed to bring a "plus one" so you can show off a good-looking date? Drink three more while planning a killer outfit and a substandard gift for the blessed event.

Bad Day: *Bad sex*

There's a saying that bad sex is better than no sex. That's always *sounded* true, but after last night, you're not so sure. All you know is that you desperately need a do-over, a chance to fix that fumbling mess that passed for sex last night. And if you can't have that, you'd like to lie down and forget it all, fast. Either way, it's time to get Between the Sheets.

Good Drink: *Between the Sheets*

> *1 ounce brandy or Cognac*
> *1 ounce light rum*
> *1 ounce Cointreau*
> *1 ounce fresh lemon juice*
> *Dash of simple syrup (see page 35)*
> *Lemon twist for garnish*

Shake the brandy, rum, Cointreau, lemon juice, and simple syrup with ice and strain into a chilled cocktail glass. Twist the lemon peel over the drink and drop it in. Drink while visualizing your more illustrious conquests.

Bad Day: *Big fight with main squeeze*

It started out as some harmless bickering, and then before you knew it, you were saying things you really wish you could take back. How could you fight like that with your beloved Sig-O? It's time to apologize—but first, a drink. (If your squeeze is still speaking to you, make another as a peace offering.)

Good Drink: *Short Fuse*

2 ounces tequila
½ ounce apricot brandy
1½ ounces fresh lime juice
3 ounces fresh grapefruit juice
¼ ounce maraschino cherry juice (from the jar of cherries)
Lime wedge

Shake the tequila, brandy, lime juice, grapefruit juice, and maraschino cherry juice with ice and strain into an ice-filled glass. Squeeze the lime wedge and drop it in. Take one swig and then kiss and make up.

Bad Day: *Worst kiss ever*

Perhaps you built it up for too long in your mind. Perhaps you were thinking too much about technique. Perhaps your expectations were too high. But wow, that was really the worst. Nothing disappoints like a really bad kiss—especially when you were sure it was going to be perfect. Time to pucker up and put your mouth on something you know will be delicious.

Good Drink: *French Kiss*

⅔ ounce raspberry purée
1 ounce ginger beer
Dash of apricot brandy
3 to 5 ounces chilled champagne
Fresh raspberries for garnish

Pour raspberry purée, ginger beer, and brandy into a chilled champagne flute and stir. Slowly add the champagne. Garnish with the raspberries, and feel free to fish them out with your tongue.

Bad Day: *Stolen date*

Sure, you knew you were taking your chances, bringing the best-looking date you've had in months to a crowded bar or party. And granted, you guys weren't exclusive or anything. You were just getting started, hoping to reel this one in. No such luck: you leave for ten minutes, tops, and find someone else putting on the moves. That bites.

Good Drink: *Barracuda*

1½ ounces gold rum
1 ounce Galliano
3 ounces pineapple juice
½ ounce fresh lime juice
Lime wedge for garnish

Shake the rum, Galliano, pineapple juice, and lime juice with ice and strain into an ice-filled highball glass. Garnish with a lime wedge. Accept that sometimes, the big ones get away.

Bad Day: *Struck out*

Man, it's been a long dry spell. Lately, no matter how hard you try, you just don't seem able to close the deal. This time you used all your charm, your best lines, and perhaps even resorted to begging—but alas, it's another no-go, and you're home alone again. What's a guy or gal to do but make a solo trip, well, South of the Border?

Good Drink: *South of the Border*

½ lime
1 ounce tequila
¾ ounce Kahlúa or Tia Maria

Squeeze the lime into a chilled glass and drop it in. Fill with ice and pour in the tequila and Kahlúa; stir.

From Bad to Worse: Even your frisky ex turned down a no-strings booty call? Double the tequila and call it a night—it's time to cut your losses.

Bad Day: *Best friend is in love*

You used to do everything together—including complaining about the opposite sex. But today, your best friend cancelled on you again, and guess why? Love. And worse yet, it's the really irritating kind. So while you're still rolling solo, you have to hear every minute detail of the newfound bliss, including their icky pet names and schmaltzy future plans. The only antidote is to sail away on a Honeymoon of your own!

Good Drink: *Honeymoon*

> *1½ ounces apple brandy*
> *¾ ounce Bénédictine*
> *¼ ounce Cointreau*
> *1 ounce fresh lemon juice*
> *Lemon twist for garnish*

Shake the brandy, Bénédictine, Cointreau, and lemon juice with ice and strain into a chilled cocktail glass. Twist the lemon peel over the drink and drop it in. Remember, loving yourself is the beginning of a lifelong relationship!

Bad Day: *Ugly breakup*

Millions of women worldwide can't be wrong: regardless of your gender, chocolate cures what ails you, especially when it comes to matters of the heart. Mix that chocolate with some good strong booze and you've got a winning therapeutic combination. And it doesn't matter whether you're the breaker or the breakee—after a few of these, you won't even remember.

Good Drink: *Death by Chocolate*

¾ ounce Baileys or other Irish cream liqueur
¾ ounce dark crème de cacao
¾ ounce vodka
¼ cup chocolate ice cream
Chocolate shavings or chocolate chips for garnish

Combine the Baileys, crème de cacao, vodka, and ice cream in
a blender with ½ cup ice. Blend until smooth, and pour into a
chilled wine glass. Garnish with chocolate shavings and indulge.

From Bad to Worse: **Is it Valentine's Day? Give yourself fifty extra pity points,
double the vodka, and supplement with a heart-shaped box of bonbons that are
all for you.**

BAD DAYS:
HOME

Bad Day: *Noisy neighbors kept you up all night*

Has another sleepless night with the obnoxious partiers next door left you squinty-eyed and surly? Before you bang on the wall with the broom handle yet again, bang out a batch of this delicious cocktail. Two tall Harvey Wallbangers, plus a handy set of earplugs, will drown out the sound like you won't believe.

Good Drink: *Harvey Wallbanger*

1½ ounces vodka
4 to 5 ounces orange juice
½ ounce Galliano

Shake the vodka and orange juice with ice, and strain into an ice-filled highball glass. Float the Galliano on top.

From Bad to Worse: **Party just starting? And the clock says 3 a.m.? Add another shot of vodka and an ice pack for your head.**

Bad Day: *Rent hike*

When your living expenses increase overnight with no warning, it can feel totally unfair. The only solace is that you're not living in Manhattan, home to the highest housing prices in the United States. (If you *are* living there, you're probably already drinking these every time you write your rent check.) So hey, you're out another couple hundred bucks. Bottoms up—it's better than moving!

Good Drink: *Manhattan*

2 ounces rye, bourbon, or blended whiskey
¾ ounce sweet vermouth
2 dashes Angostura bitters
Maraschino cherry for garnish

Stir the whiskey, vermouth, and bitters with ice. Strain into a chilled cocktail glass. Garnish with the cherry.

From Bad to Worse: Building is going co-op? Replace the maraschino cherry with seven brandied cherries, then start planning the blowout party you're going to have at your pad before moving somewhere better.

Bad Day: *Household disaster*

The toilet's backed up. The washer overflowed. The IKEA furniture you spent all day putting together is missing three essential pieces. And although you're sure you own a toolbox, you have no idea where it is. Chances are, on a day like this, no one is answering your call for help . . . so sit back and survey the damage with a delicious drink that's hard to screw up.

Good Drink: *Rusty Nail*

1½ ounces Scotch
1 ounce Drambuie
Lemon twist for garnish

Pour the Scotch and Drambuie into an ice-filled old-fashioned glass and stir. Twist the lemon over the drink and drop it in.

Bad Day: *Cable on the fritz*

Chances are, it's happened on the day of the big game, a movie marathon you've been waiting for, or the season premiere of your favorite show—leaving you staring helplessly at a screen full of fuzz. Did you forget to pay the bill? Did someone figure out you've been getting cable for free? Is someone playing a terrible joke on you? And does a live body *ever* answer when you call the cable company? Ponder these burning questions over a couple of these elaborate cocktails, and even the static might start to look interesting. (Don't let the number of ingredients put you off—you've got nothing to do anyway!)

Good Drink: *Zombie*

1 ounce light rum
1 ounce gold rum
1 ounce dark rum
½ ounce apricot brandy
1 ounce crème de banana
1 ounce pineapple juice
1 ounce fresh lemon juice
1 ounce fresh lime juice
¼ ounce grenadine
1 tablespoon brown sugar
½ ounce 151-proof rum
Pineapple wedge, lime wheel, and cherry for garnish

Shake the light rum, gold rum, dark rum, brandy, crème de banana, pineapple juice, lemon juice, lime juice, grenadine, and brown sugar with ice and strain into an ice-filled highball glass. Float the 151-proof rum on top. Garnish with the fruit.

Bad Day: *Cleaning day*

Whether it's a once-a-year spring cleaning, a mountain of laundry that can no longer be ignored, or a top-to-bottom scrubbing because of a possible overnight guest (or all three!), it's hard to get psyched up for cleaning. What's the right way to get motivated? Tackle the dirty work with a similarly filthy little cocktail.

Good Drink: *Dirty Martini*

2 ounces gin
½ ounce extra-dry vermouth
½ ounce brine from cocktail olives
Green cocktail olive for garnish

Stir the gin, vermouth, and brine in a mixing glass with ice and strain into a chilled cocktail glass (a dirty one will do). Garnish with the olive.

Bad Day: *Cranky relatives staying with you*

They demand breakfast. They insist on watching *their* TV shows. They even want your bed! Whether it's your parents, your crazy sister, or your out-of-work uncle, sharing your pad with annoying relatives is the worst. It cramps your style, makes you eager to be at the office, and may even make you wish you were an orphan. Time to break out a potent painkiller.

Good Drink: *Quaalude*

1 ounce vodka
1 ounce hazelnut liqueur
1 ounce coffee liqueur
1 splash milk

Pour the vodka, hazelnut liqueur, coffee liqueur, and milk into an old-fashioned glass filled with ice, and serve — to yourself, not your guests!

From Bad to Worse: **Are you sleeping on the couch, uncomfortable sofa bed, or air mattress? Add a shot of Baileys in place of the milk.**

Bad Day: *Moving day*

You're surrounded by bubble wrap, old newspaper, and not nearly enough boxes—and, of course, your friends who promised to help are nowhere in sight. How are you going to lift all this stuff? Where's the tape gun buried? Did you pack all the pens you own? Hopefully, in the midst of this chaos, you can dig up at least one glass, coffee mug, or water bottle to mix this drink in—because what you need right now, my friend, is some magic.

Good Drink: *Black Magic*

1½ ounces vodka
¾ ounce Kahlúa or Tia Maria
Dash of fresh lemon juice
Lemon twist for garnish

Shake the vodka, Kahlúa, and lemon juice with ice and strain
into an ice-filled glass. Twist the lemon peel over the drink and
drop it in. Say "abracadabra" and visualize all your stuff float-
ing merrily to its new home.

**From Bad to Worse: Still have to clean your old place once you're done?
Make it a double!**

Bad Day: *Screwed over by roommate*

Okay, you live with the antichrist. You have a long list of complaints, but today was the last straw. Did your roommate ruin your favorite cashmere sweater, scare your date, sleep in your bed, dirty every dish in the house, drink your best bottle of wine, break the toilet, or forget to pay yet another important bill? Regardless of the offense this time, face it: you've been screwed over. Turn your stress back a notch with this essential tool.

Good Drink: *Screwdriver*

2 ounces vodka
4 to 6 ounces orange juice
Orange wheel for garnish

Pour the vodka and orange juice into an ice-filled highball
glass and stir. Garnish with the orange and hide in your room.

Bad Day: *Actually home sick on sick day*

You've been looking forward to this sick day. You started fake-coughing at work two days ago, practiced your scratchy voice for the phone call, and planned all sorts of fun ways to enjoy a much-deserved day of hooky. But now—disaster!—you find you're actually sick and stuck at home. It's a cruel punishment, but it does give you the excuse to make a delicious, restorative drink that might actually cure what ails you—so you can have a better sick day next time. To your health!

Good Drink: *Blueberry Tea*

1 ounce Grand Marnier
1 ounce amaretto
Hot orange pekoe or Earl Grey tea to taste
Lemon wheel for garnish

Pour the Grand Marnier and amaretto into a warm mug or brandy snifter. Add hot tea to taste and garnish with the lemon wheel. Find slippers, flip on daytime TV, and commence feeling sorry for yourself.

Bad Day: *Party aftermath*

It seemed like a good idea at the time: a few friends over for a little party at your place. But somehow a harmless get-together turned into a full-on blow-out, and you're left picking up the pieces today. The couch is stained, the carpet is rank, icky remnants of last night's food and drink are everywhere—and you don't even want to look in the bathroom. Before you deal with this disaster, take a moment to open a couple of windows, breathe some fresh air, and sip a drink that will temporarily transport you to a sweeter, more civilized place.

Good Drink: *Sea Breeze*

1½ ounces vodka
3 ounces grapefruit juice
2 ounces cranberry juice
Lime wedge

Pour the vodka, grapefruit juice, and cranberry juice into an ice-filled highball glass and stir. Squeeze the lime over the drink and drop it in.

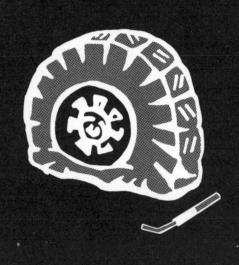

BAD DAYS:
LIFE IN
GENERAL

Bad Day: *Car broke down*

Looks like you're going to be bus-bound for a while. Cheer up: Think of all the interesting characters you'll meet! How much faster your commute will be in the bus lane! How much better for the environment it is to not drive your own vehicle! Okay, okay, it still sucks. Pour yourself a refreshing beverage, toast your car, and pray that the mechanic doesn't make things worse.

Good Drink: *Greyhound*

2 ounces vodka
5 ounces fresh grapefruit juice

Pour the vodka and grapefruit juice into an ice-filled highball glass and stir.

Bad Day: *Flight cancelled*

Travel can be a nightmare, from security lines to bad food to lost luggage. But when you get to the airport two hours early, toting a tiny carry-on, and endure an interminable wait only to be told it's not going to happen? Doesn't matter if it's a mechanical snafu or a legitimate "act of God," it feels like a disaster—and you deserve a powerful drink to whip things back into shape.

Good Drink: *Hurricane*

1½ ounces dark rum
1 ounce light rum
½ ounce passion fruit juice
1½ ounces orange juice
1 ounce lime juice
1 ounce pineapple juice
Dash of Angostura bitters
Lime and pineapple wedges for garnish

Shake the dark rum, light rum, passion fruit juice, orange juice, lime juice, pineapple juice, and bitters vigorously with ice. Strain into an ice-filled glass. Garnish with the lime and pineapple wedges. Serve packets of dry-roasted peanuts on the side, and drink in front of the Weather Channel to make yourself feel better.

From Bad to Worse: **No flights leaving for at least forty-eight hours? Double the rum and serve in a hurricane glass for the classic high-octane Hurricane.**

Bad Day: *Fashion faux pas*

Why didn't your friends warn you? Somehow, you wore your best cocktail attire when everyone else was in graphic T's, or worse, you sported jeans and a hoodie when the whole place was decked out. If the evening included an impeccably dressed date who looked downright horrified when you walked in, it's time to lose yourself in a color-coordinated drink that's always in style.

Good Drink: *Black and Tan*

8 ounces Guinness or other stout
8 ounces pale ale or lager

Pour the Guinness into a pint glass and slowly top with the pale ale. Admire the classic lines and timeless palette before quaffing.

Bad Day: *Got arrested*

Whoops! You got taken down to the station. Surely there was some sort of mix-up regarding that suspended license, barroom brawl, tax return, or public display of drunkenness, and all will be straightened out quickly. But once you've been fingerprinted, you can no longer order sissy drinks. After you post bail, order up this one.

Good Drink: *Alabama Slammer*

1 ounce Southern Comfort
1 ounce amaretto
½ ounce sloe gin
1 ounce orange juice

Shake the Southern Comfort, amaretto, gin, and orange juice
with ice and strain into an ice-filled glass.

From Bad to Worse: Actually spend the night in the slammer? Skip the ice and
pour the ingredients into a tall shot glass; knock it back like the badass you are.

Bad Day: *Called "sir" or "ma'am" by teenage salesclerk*

If there's anything more annoying than an inept teenage salesperson, it's an inept teenage salesperson who acts like you're old. You! Old? As if! When they say "sir" or "ma'am" in that bratty voice, speak very slowly to you, or expect you to not understand any high-tech terms, it's time to prove that you can beat those kids at their own game. No matter what year you graduated from high school (and *no one* needs to know), you can still party with the best of them!

Good Drink: *Vodka Red Bull*

2 ounces vodka
10 ounces Red Bull

Pour the vodka and Red Bull into an ice-filled glass and stir. Quickly follow with a different, grown-up drink to get the horrible taste out of your mouth.

From Bad to Worse: **Dissed by youngsters while at a bar? Order this as a Depth Charge, with the shot of vodka dropped into the glass of Red Bull. Chug! Chug! Chug!**

Bad Day: *Totally unfair speeding ticket*

Okay, maybe you were going a wee bit over the speed limit, but was it your fault you had an 8 a.m. meeting to get to? You were only trying to be responsible. And if that humorless police officer had time to join you for this drink, surely he would've come around to your point of view. In the meantime, move into the "sloe" lane and put away your keys; it's cocktail hour.

Good Drink: *Sloe Gin Fizz*

2 ounces sloe gin
1½ ounces fresh lemon juice
½ ounce simple syrup (see page 35)
3 to 4 ounces chilled club soda
Maraschino cherry for garnish

Shake the gin, lemon juice, and simple syrup with ice. Strain into an ice-filled highball glass, then top with club soda and stir. Garnish with the cherry.

From Bad to Worse: **Not your first moving violation this year? If you can look forward to an insurance rate hike, a Sloe Screw is also appropriate: just mix equal parts of sloe gin and orange juice over ice.**

Bad Day: *Hangover*

It doesn't matter how many you've had in your lifetime, a bad hangover is . . . bad. Really, really bad. Your head is splitting, your belly is flip-flopping, the room is spinning, and your teeth are wearing little furry sweaters. How could you have let this happen? When will you ever learn? Ah, cut yourself a break. Shuffle into the kitchen for a simple hangover remedy that matches your current bloodshot look.

Good Drink: *Red Eye*

3 ounces tomato juice
12 ounces beer (ale or lager)

Pour the tomato juice into a chilled beer mug, and slowly add the beer. Drink slowly while turning the volume down on all appliances in the house.

Bad Day: *Buyer's remorse*

It still hasn't quite sunk in. You wake up early thinking maybe
it was a dream, but then you check the credit card receipts —
and yes, you really blew through all that dough. Maybe it was
one big-ticket item like a snowboard, fancy shoes, a leather
couch, or a flat-screen TV. Maybe it was just an innocent spree
that somehow took on a life of its own. Either way, you are left
feeling queasy. Time to pour yourself something light, bubbly,
and refreshing to celebrate keeping the economy afloat!

Good Drink: *Mimosa*

2 ounces fresh orange juice
3 to 5 ounces chilled champagne

Pour the orange juice into a chilled champagne flute. Top slowly with champagne and stir gently. Say, "I deserve it!"

From Bad to Worse: Over your limit on more than one credit card? Add ¼ ounce of Cointreau to the orange juice before topping with the bubbly.

Bad Day: *Tax day*

Of all the days that the U.S. government seems like it's out to get you, this might take the cake—taxes. You know what they say: you can't escape them. How can you possibly hand over so much money every two weeks and *still* owe a fortune in April? It's time for a liberating drink, something to make you feel free and unshackled, if only for a night. Invite some other disgruntled Americans over for a simple, inexpensive cocktail that helped fuel a revolution.

Good Drink: *Cuba Libre*

½ lime
2 ounces light rum
4 to 6 ounces chilled cola
Lime wedge for garnish

Squeeze the lime into an ice-filled highball glass and drop it in.
Add the rum, top with the cola, and garnish with the lime wedge.

Bad Day: *Gained weight*

Lately, you've been feeling a bit . . . well, weightier than normal.
The tailor seems to have incorrectly altered your favorite pants,
and all of your T-shirts have mysteriously shrunk in the dryer.
If you've finally dug out your scale and discovered the awful
truth, you probably need a drink. And forget that club soda
crap; you need a real drink, a calorie-laden bullet, a celebratory
shot that lets you properly welcome your newfound pounds.
After three of these, you'll realize you were actually too skinny
before. Bigger is better!

Good Drink: *Butterball*

½ ounce vodka
½ ounce Baileys or other Irish cream liqueur
½ ounce butterscotch schnapps

Pour the vodka, Baileys, and butterscotch schnapps into a chilled shot glass. Knock it back.

From Bad to Worse: **Did the scale go up more than ten pounds? Indulge in a heavy cream floater!**

Bad Day: *Sold out by friend*

Et tu, Brutus? Maybe your "pal" gave you the opposite shoulder tap while the boss was offering up box seats. Maybe she sneakily scored the apartment you'd been eyeing and then acted innocent. Maybe he offered your date a ride home while you were buying the next round. Whatever the reason for the treason, getting sold up the river by a supposed friend always stings. So commiserate with a guy who really got dinged, and relax . . . unlike him, you'll live to fight another day. Onward!

Good Drink: *Bloody Caesar*

2 ounces vodka
4 ounces Clamato juice
½ ounce fresh lemon juice
¼ teaspoon horseradish
2 to 3 dashes Tabasco sauce
2 to 3 dashes Worcestershire sauce
Lemon wedge
Celery stick or pickled asparagus for garnish

Shake the vodka, Clamato juice, lemon juice, horseradish, Tabasco, and Worcestershire with ice and strain into an ice-filled highball glass. Squeeze the lemon wedge over the drink and drop it in. Garnish with the celery.

Bad Day: *Got into a fight*

Found yourself embroiled in a knock-down, drag-out fight? Sometimes, push really does come to shove and there's no turning back. Surely, the other guy (or gal) deserved it. Whether fists actually flew, or just some heated words and a lamp, you deserve some TLC to recover. If you lick your wounds and then make this drink, you'll have a one-two punch guaranteed to make you feel better.

Good Drink: *Planter's Punch*

2 ounces dark rum
Dash of Cointreau
1½ ounces fresh orange juice
1½ ounces pineapple juice
½ ounce fresh lime juice
½ ounce simple syrup (see page 35)
Dash of grenadine
Orange wheel and maraschino cherry for garnish

Shake the rum, Cointreau, orange juice, pineapple juice, lime juice, simple syrup, and grenadine with ice and strain into an ice-filled highball glass. Garnish with the orange wheel and cherry. Serve with ice pack if needed.

From Bad to Worse: **Was the fight idiotic and totally your fault? Call to apologize— and invite your enemy over for another round (of drinks, that is).**

Bad Day: *Crummy birthday*

No gifts left on your doorstep? No surprise party at the local pub? Even your *own parents* forgot to call? What the hell? You deserve better than this after another successful year of life on this planet. Close the blinds, light some candles, and get the party started with this decadent and delicious cake substitute. Happy birthday to you!

Good Drink: *Irish Cream Milkshake*

2 scoops vanilla ice cream
1 cup milk
Baileys or other Irish cream liqueur to taste
Whipped cream, chocolate syrup, and/or mint leaves for garnish

Blend ice cream, milk, and a large splash of Baileys in a blender with ice. Add more Baileys as desired. Pour into a chilled glass and top with whipped cream, a drizzle of chocolate syrup, and mint leaves. Make a wish for a better birthday next year!

From Bad to Worse: Was it a "milestone birthday" to boot? Add a shot of vodka, coffee liqueur, or both—and drink while buying yourself a kick-ass present online.

Bad Day: *Painful grooming treatment*

Sometimes, you've got to bite the bullet in the name of looking good, especially if there's a special occasion looming. If today you've endured something that was physically painful (like the waxing of a body part) or psychologically traumatic (like a truly heinous haircut) you deserve a little post-treatment anesthetic to take the edge off.

Good Drink: *Fuzzy Navel*

2 ounces peach schnapps
4 ounces orange juice
Orange wheel or peach slice for garnish

Shake the peach schnapps and orange juice with ice and strain into an ice-filled glass. Garnish with the fruit.

From Bad to Worse: **Besides the pain, are the results less than perfect? And do you have no choice but to show them off tonight? Go all out and make it a Hairy Navel by adding 1 ounce vodka.**

Bad Day: *Sports team got crushed*

What a heartbreaking display by your favorite team. It was almost too painful to watch! Whether you were in the stands, in front of the TV, or actually on the field, it hurts. It really, really hurts. If you find yourself fighting back tears, disguise them quickly with a salty, soothing drink that's named for man's best friend — someone who *doesn't* let you down. Make a round of these and reminisce about the glory days.

Good Drink: *Salty Dog*

Lemon wedge
Salt for rimming glass
2 ounces vodka
4 to 6 ounces grapefruit juice

Rub the rim of a chilled highball glass with the lemon wedge and coat with salt. Fill the glass with ice, pour in the vodka and grapefruit juice, and stir. Squeeze the lemon over the drink and drop it in.

From Bad to Worse: Have more than fifty bucks riding on this debacle? Make it a double and cut the juice in half.

Bad Day: *Miserable weather*

It's been pouring for days. No, weeks. Months, maybe? You open the blinds in the morning and all you want to do is get back into bed. You feel damp, chilled, and downright depressed—and it's only going to get worse. Sleet, slush, and icy roads are on the horizon! If you can't escape to a sunny clime for the season, you might as well wallow in it. Put on your Wellies, splash in some puddles, then come inside to enjoy a different kind of storm front.

Good Drink: *Dark and Stormy*

1 to 2 slices fresh ginger (optional)
2 ounces dark rum
½ tablespoon ginger syrup or simple syrup (see page 35)
3 to 4 ounces ginger beer
2 lime wedges

Fill a glass with ice and add the fresh ginger, if using. Add
the rum and ginger syrup and stir. Top with the ginger beer.
Squeeze the lime wedges and drop them in. Drink next to a
space heater or sunlamp.

Bad Day: *Last-minute holiday shopping*

Why are the holidays so maddening? The traffic is awful, there's nowhere to park, the salesclerks are cranky, and the other shoppers are quite literally manic. You almost broke your wrist wrestling the last cashmere scarf—which you clearly saw first—out of a mean old lady's death grip! Granted, you may have waited a tad bit too long to shop this year, but still. Put the bags away, ignore the Christmas cards waiting to be addressed, and have some hot buttered holiday cheer.

Good Drink: *Hot Buttered Rum*

1 teaspoon brown sugar
4 ounces hot water
2 ounces dark rum or bourbon
1 tablespoon butter
Freshly grated nutmeg for garnish

In a warmed mug, combine the brown sugar and hot water, stirring until sugar is dissolved. Add the rum and float the butter on top. Sprinkle with nutmeg.

From Bad to Worse: Still have more than five presents to buy? Add an extra rum floater!

Bad Day: *Fender bender*

Whether you or the other idiot were to blame, a fender bender is a hassle for both parties. With the insurance issues, unsightly dents, and evil mechanics, one way or another you're always out more dough than you ever expected. How can a Toyota bumper cost two grand? This calls for a drink named for a barfly who cleverly chose not to drive, instead being chauffeured nightly in a motorcycle sidecar.

Good Drink: *Sidecar*

Lemon wedge
Sugar for rimming glass
1½ ounces Cognac or brandy
¾ ounce Cointreau or triple sec
¾ ounce fresh lemon juice
Lemon twist for garnish

Rub the rim of a cocktail glass with the lemon wedge and coat with sugar. Shake the Cognac, Cointreau, and lemon juice with ice and strain into the glass. Twist the lemon peel over the drink and drop it in.

INDEX

Absinthe, 7
Alabama Slammer, 85
Ale, 83, 91
Amaretto, 33, 73, 85
Angostura bitters, 39, 59, 81
Apple brandy, 51
Apricot brandy, 43, 45, 63
B-52, 5
Baileys Irish Cream
    B-52, 5
    Butterball, 97
    Death by Chocolate, 53
    Irish Cream
        Milkshake, 103
    Mudslide, 17
    Quaalude, 67
Barracuda, 47
Beautiful, 33
Beer, 83, 91
Bellini, 45
Benedictine, 51
Between the Sheets, 41
Bitters, Angostura, 39, 59, 81
Black and Tan, 83
Black Magic, 69
Blended drinks
    Blue Hawaiian, 15
    Death by Chocolate, 53
    Mudslide, 17
Bloody Caesar, 99
Blue Curaçao, 15
Blue Hawaiian, 15
Blueberry Tea, 73
Bourbon
    Hot Buttered Rum, 111
    Hot Toddy, 21
    Manhattan, 59
Brandy, 13, 41, 113
Brandy, apple, 51
Brandy, apricot, 43, 45, 63
Butterball, 97
Butterscotch schnapps, 97
Chambord, 31, 37
Champagne
    Bellini, 25
    Champagne Cocktail, 39
    French 75, 29

French Kiss, 45
    Mimosa, 93
    Death in the Afternoon, 7
Champagne Cocktail, 39
Cherry juice, maraschino, 43
Chocolate ice cream, 53
Clamato juice, 99
Cloves, 11, 21
Club soda, 9, 19, 31, 89
Coconut, cream of, 15
Coffee drinks
    Flaming Diablo, 11
    Irish Coffee, 3
Coffee liqueur, 67, 103
Cognac
    Beautiful, 33
    Between the Sheets, 41
    Flaming Diablo, 11
    Sidecar, 113
Cointreau
    Flaming Diablo, 11
    Honeymoon, 51
    Kamikaze, 23
    Mimosa, 93
    Planter's Punch, 101
    Sidecar, 113
Cola, 95
Cranberry juice, 37, 75
Cream of coconut, 15
Cream, heavy, 3, 17, 97
Crème de banana, 63
Crème de cacao, 53
Crème de menthe, 13, 19
Cuba Libre, 95
Curaçao, 15
Dark and Stormy, 109
Death by Chocolate, 53
Death in the Afternoon, 7
Dirty Martini, 65
Drambuie, 61
Earl Gray tea, 73
Flaming Diablo, 11
French 75, 29
French Kiss, 45
Fuzzy Navel, 105
Galliano, 47, 57
Garnishes, ix

Gin
    Dirty Martini, 65
    French 75, 29
    Greenback, 19
Ginger beer, 45, 109
Ginger syrup, 109
Ginger, fresh, 109
Glassware, viii–ix
Grand Marnier, 5, 33, 73
Grapefruit juice, 43, 75,
    79, 107
Greenback, 19
Grenadine, 31, 63, 101
Greyhound, 79
Guinness, 83
Hairy Navel, 105
Harvey Wallbanger, 57
Hazelnut liqueur, 67
Heavy cream, 3, 17, 97
Honeymoon, 51
Horseradish, 99
Hot Buttered Rum, 111
Hot drinks, 3, 11, 21, 73, 111
Hot Toddy, 21
Hurricane, 81
Ice cream
    Chocolate, 53
    Vanilla, 103
Irish Coffee, 3
Irish cream liqueur
    B-52, 5
    Butterball, 97
    Death by Chocolate, 53
    Irish Cream
        Milkshake, 103
    Mudslide, 17
    Quaalude, 67
Irish Cream Milkshake, 103
Kahlua
    B-52, 5
    Black Magic, 69
    Mind Eraser, 9
    Mudslide, 17
    South of the Border, 49
Kamikaze, 23
Lager, 83, 91
Lemon, 21, 107, 113

Lemon juice, 29, 35, 41, 51,
   63, 69, 89, 99, 113
Lemon peel, 11
Lemon-flavored vodka, 37
Lime, 49, 75, 95, 109
Lime juice, 19, 23, 43, 47, 63,
   81, 101
Love Potion, 37
Manhattan, 59
Maraschino cherry juice, 43
Milk, 67, 103
Mimosa, 93
Mind Eraser, 9
Mudslide, 17
Olives, cocktail, 65
Orange juice, 31, 57, 71, 81,
   85, 89, 93, 101, 105
Orange pekoe tea, 73
Pale ale, 83
Passion fruit juice, 81
Peach nectar, 25
Peach puree, 25
Peach schnapps, 105
Peppermint schnapps, 13
Pernod, 7
Pineapple juice, 15, 47, 63,
   81, 101
Planter's Punch, 101
Prosecco, 25
Quaalude, 67
Raspberry puree, 45
Red Bull, 87
Red Eye, 91
Rum
   Barracuda, 47
   Between the Sheets, 41
   Blue Hawaiian, 15
   Cuba Libre, 95

Dark and Stormy, 109
Hot Buttered Rum, 111
Hurricane, 81
Planter's Punch, 101
Zombie, 63
Rum, 151-proof, 63
Rusty Nail, 61
Rye, 59
Salty Dog, 107
Schnapps
   butterscotch, 97
   peach, 105
   peppermint, 13
Scotch, 61
Screwdriver, 71
Sea Breeze, 75
Short Fuse, 43
Sidecar, 113
Simple syrup,
   instructions, 35
Sloe gin, 85, 89
Sloe Gin Fizz, 89
Sloe Screw, 89
South of the Border, 49
Southern Comfort, 85
Sparkling wine, 25
Stinger, 13
Stout, 83
Tabasco sauce, 99
Tea, 11, 73
Tequila
   Short Fuse, 43
   South of the Border, 49
   Tequila Sunrise, 31
Tequila Sunrise, 31
Tia Maria, 49, 69
Tomato juice, 91
Triple sec, 23, 113

Vanilla ice cream, 103
Vermouth, 59, 65
Vodka
   Black Magic, 69
   Bloody Caesar, 99
   Butterball, 97
   Death by Chocolate, 53
   Fuzzy Navel, 105
   Greyhound, 79
   Hairy Navel, 105
   Harvey Wallbanger, 57
   Irish Cream
      Milkshake, 103
   Kamikaze, 23
   Love Potion, 37
   Mind Eraser, 9
   Mudslide, 17
   Quaalude, 67
   Salty Dog, 107
   Screwdriver, 71
   Sea Breeze, 75
   Stinger, 13
   Vodka Red Bull, 87
   White Spider Stinger, 13
Vodka, lemon-flavored, 37
Vodka Red Bull, 87
Whipped cream, 3
Whiskey
   Irish Coffee, 3
   Manhattan, 59
   Whiskey Sour, 35
Whiskey, blended, 59
Whiskey, Irish, 3
Whiskey Sour, 35
White Spider Stinger, 13
Wine, sparkling, 25
Worcestershire sauce, 99
Zombie, 63

About the Author

Kerry Colburn is a freelance writer who lives and drinks in Seattle, where her family, friends, and well-stocked bar guard against foul moods. She's the author of several books, including *The U.S. of Eh?: How Canada Secretly Controls the United States*, which she co-authored with her husband, Rob Sorensen.